I Wish Someone Told Me...

Christie Jones

BookLeaf Publishing

Presentation by *BookLeaf Publishing*

Web: www.bookleafpub.com

E-mail: info@bookleafpub.com

ISBN: 9789357440400

First edition 2023

DEDICATION

To J.B. - I wish you were here to see this!

ACKNOWLEDGEMENT

I have wanted to be an author since as long as I can remember. Over the years, I allowed that dream to get pushed aside for other dreams and other career goals. But writing never left me and I always looked to writing poetry as a way to journal. I still had a small, vague hope that I would someday be able to publish my own book but it didn't become a reality without the help of so many people. Firstly, I do need to thank my friend Holly, who steered me onto Bookleaf Publishing. Holly has always encouraged me to follow my dreams and I want to take this moment to say thank you and I couldn't have done so much of this without her support.

I also want to thank my mother (rest in peace) for giving me the poetry bug. Growing up, I remember reading my mothers poems and wanting to write like she did. My mother had a gift for rhyme that I don't have, and wish I did. Her poems were never published and sadly most of them got lost over the years. She never thought writing would be a solid career choice for me (too competitive), but I feel her with me still as I publish this. I chose to include poems to honor both of my parents and I also want to take a moment to acknowledge them both here for their love and support over the years. They never encouraged me to be an author, but they always encouraged me to do my best and for that I am grateful.

For all others who have been a part of me getting here, Nancy, Stephanie, John, Tom, Marla, Lynn, and anyone I'm forgetting to mention, I thank you all and am grateful to have you in my life.

Winter

Winter here is cold and bitter,
such a lonely place to be.
Isolated in silence,
with only myself unseen.
Whiteness all around me,
as far as the eyes can see.
Winter is a season;
it will pass like all the rest.
But the stillness of the silence,
the starkness of the snow,
show us who we are inside,
when there's no where else to go.
There is beauty in the quiet,
warmth within the cold.
And loneliness is only just a word.

Still I Rise.

Days of sadness, nights of pain,
no one understands who I am.
Fearing nothing will change.
A scream, I always hold back.

Loneliness surrounds me, fear in my heart,
told I'm nothing, told I'm apart.
To overcome all these feelings of pain,
there must be more than they perceive.

Finding strength, finding peace,
I feel I can never achieve.
I search and I search and I start to find,
to learn, to value, to love what's inside.

Day by day, I continue to strive,
to work and learn to be all that I am.
Overcoming those who didn't believe
Knowing that I can only seek.

Today is no different,
than days of the past.
Loneliness, success, love and the rest.
I take it all in because that's who I am.

I hurt, I love, I value, I care.
Shame, guilt, worry and fear.
All of this, is who I shall be,
it matters not, the road was heavy.

For all that I learned was that
I can survive.
I hurt and I fear, I learn and I love.
It matters not, for each day that passes.

I face the pain,
I feel the fear,
I give the love,
So still I rise.

Faces

What do I show thee?
Let me count the ways.
A happy face,
can tell a lie,
to those who do not see.
But then again,
what is truth,
what emotions are real?
A frown can mean
many things,
not just what it seems.
A face to others,
what they glimpse,
is in ways up to them.
For I may show them me,
but then they look away.
So, faces that we
show the world
are not the truth by far.
For truth is just an illusion,
not who we really are.

Kryptonite

A glowing green rock,
brings strength to its knees.
His power knows no more.
He cannot fly, he cannot save
the world from evil no more.
What then affects you and I?
What is your own private hell?
A solid rock, glowing with green,
or something you cannot see.
Deep within our souls we fight,
our weakness, our own cross to bear.
Definitely, that which makes you weak,
gives it more power to snare.
On worry, on doubt, fear and on angst,
maybe all the above.
My own glowing green rock
may change from here and beyond.
How I live and how I show
others who I am.
I keep that glowing green rock,
buried beneath the sand.
It creeps out from time to time,
and brings me to my knees.
I struggle, cry and rage,
until I can stand with ease.

For allowing that glowing rock to
dominate my core,
gives it all the power it seeks,
to destroy us all.
To overcome, to conquer,
this I seek each day,
and one day
that damn green rock
will break and drift away.

Ocean Breezes

Ocean breezes
calm my mind,
and bring some clarity.
The roaring surf,
the diamond waves,
take all my pain away.
I see the people,
the small children,
puppies in the sand.
The happy smiles,
the gentle wind,
gives life from the despair.
I look into the blue abyss,
far as my eyes can see.
I don't know
how to explain,
the peace it brings to me.

Beyond Despair

Haunted by the stories I hear,
the pain I see each day.
Years and years
of listening to those,
who suffer,
say words of pain.
The hurt they feel,
beyond despair,
no one can understand.
All I can do,
is let them know,
I listen and I care.
I try until it gets too hard,
my mind and heart burnt out.
Weariness engulfs empathy,
of this there is no doubt.
How to find my inner calm,
allowing me to know,
that the work I put
my heart into,
won't end up breaking my soul.

Abyss

I walked along an endless path,
looking neither left nor right.
I did not care when darkness fell,
for there was never any light.

I try to forget my ugly life,
to find some inner peace,
Always in pain, like from a knife,
nowhere to find a release.

My mind is filled with bitter thoughts,
I look and search the sky above.
There is no moon, no stars to see,
as empty as a life with no love.

I have never known such abyss,
a hopeless life to lead.
No place to find, no way home,
I tried, so please forgive me.

I Wish Someone Told Me...

I wish someone told me,
that life would be so hard.
Oh, wait they did tell me,
but I was too young to see.

It started out all right.
This thing that they call life.
Happy times, sunny days,
then one day came the rain.

I wish someone told me,
how to deal with pain.
So that when the rain comes,
I can make it go away.

Feelings come and feelings go,
just like the sun and rain
But if someone had told me,
I might have learned a way.

People did say, life's not fair.
Which doesn't seem enough.
When hard times come, to hear those words,
is meaningless and rough.

I wish someone had told me,
everything will be okay.
Oh wait, that's right they did,
but believe them, there was no way.

Traveling on my own,
through this journey they call life.
I realize "wishing someone told me",
is just a way to deny.

Learning how to live,
and learning how to cope.
No one can tell me,
I must learn to find some hope.

Tell the World

If I could
tell the world
just one thing,
it would be
to listen to each other.
To sit in silence,
to not react.
We spend our days,
scrolling through
a feed.
We do not look
beyond our screens,
we blame each other,
when we don't agree.
To so many,
it is this or that,
black or white,
no grey in between.
For when we
only see one side,
we cease
to understand.
We blame each other,
for our differences

and never recognize.
That those clashes
and our struggles
only lead to dislike.
But if we were to sit in silence,
listen and reflect,
we may find some common ground,
to work our way around.
So, if I could
tell this world
one thing above all else.
It would be
to not judge
what we have
no capacity to perceive.
For in this world,
we only listen
to react.
Never to realize.

If There Were No Words...

If there were no words,
only silence,
what then would we hear?
The wind in the tress,
the cars on the road,
the rustle of falling leaves.

If there were no words,
no way to know,
how else could we hear?
Our heart beating in our chest.
Silence pressing through,
creating all we fear.

If there were no words,
but eyes to see,
what would be our view?
This world,
cloaked in quiet,
showing the way through.

If there were no words,
would you know,
could you read my soul?
Of what I want, but

cannot find,
a way to vocalize.

If there were no words,
would you see,
the way I look at you.
The sidelong glances,
the silent gestures,
my heart reveals to you.

For there are no words,
or ways to say, to show
you my whole heart.
But those words are
buried deep,
to never speak once more.

A Safe Haven

A long, long hallway,
filled with stories,
which can never be told.
Colorful quilts,
windows of light,
a sanctuary from fear.
Laughing children,
mother's braveness,
balances of anguish.
A feeling of hope,
some feelings of dread,
of what is to come.
A Safe Haven
is not forever,
we only wish it was.
Choices are made;
lives are changed.
The same,
maybe better,
maybe worse…

A Secret Place

I know of a place,
a secret place,
where love itself is stored.
A feeling that grows, and never
dies.
This place is mine alone.
No one can take this place away,
it cannot be stolen or sold.
We all have this secret place,
but not all of us know.
The place where all love is,
fills coldness in our minds.
We are blessed with this special place,
if we are lucky to survive.
I know of a place.
A secret place,
for it is called our heart.

Another Ride

The last time I spoke to mom,
I forgot to say, “I love you”.
Not saying those three words,
has haunted me for eons.
So, every time I spoke to you,
I made sure those words were said.
“I love you, Dad.”
What did that mean?
Through all those years of strife.
All the anger and impatience,
at the lack of acceptance.
For I remember all those years,
when you were my hero.
When and how did that change,
to anger and frustration?
I’ll never forget at age seven,
when I was too short for Space Mountain.
You took me to another ride,
and that’s all I remember.
Me steering that go-kart,
while you pressed the pedals,
is the earliest memory of a time
that I knew I was loved.
Growing up was hard to do,
with a parent that was hard to please.

For every happy go-kart memory,
there were two more that made me wince.
Hearing I wasn't good enough,
made to feel inferior.
Knowing I was different,
but made to feel that was wrong.
Yet, another memory pops through.
The day I asked what song to dance to.
"Always on my Mind" you said,
and made my heart shine through.
Back and forth, back and forth.
Good and bad, good and bad.
I never knew where I stood,
so, I finally stepped away.
I tried so hard to please you,
I forgot to be me.
Stepping away was hard to do.
For no one understood.
That finding and accepting myself,
couldn't include you.
I knew the chance I was taking;
I knew it probably hurt you.
And as I sit here trying to honor you;
all I can see is feeding the ducks,
balancing on the log,
learning about golf,
backyard barbeques,
dancing at my wedding,
hugging me after mom died.

And when I finally got my masters,
hearing those four words.
"I'm proud of you."
For you see that was all,
I ever wanted to hear.
I knew you loved me,
we always remembered
to say those three words.
But somewhere along the way,
we forgot to be proud.
I sit here now and think of the man,
who kept that tissue paper wreath.
For 30 years, you hung that on your door every Christmas.
That is not a man, who is not proud of his daughter.
So much time that we spent focusing on the wrong.
Now I will sit and focus, only on what's right.
From here on out,
I will remember, the father that you were.
The human being who wasn't perfect,
but did the best he could.
Wherever you are, I hope you know
how much you mean to me.
And that forever more, I will remember,
the father, who took his crying daughter
to another ride.

Night

The dark black night
fills my heart.
Gripping, squeezing,
short, rasping breaths.
Shadows surround me,
coldness overwhelms me.
In the pitch black of the night.
there is no calm
no rationale,
no candle to light my way.
My hands are ice,
my shoulders knots,
my mind has gone away.
I fall to my knees,
I cry out,
Can you see me?
Please hear me!
I need you to show me the light.
Beyond my eyes
I see a flash,
a flicker beneath my lids.
I open my eyes,
I see, I hear
the morning has finally arrived.

Fear

Sound asleep,
things are well,
dreaming in the night.
A sudden burst,
of unknown,
hurtles into my mind.
A pounding heart,
racing thoughts,
gripping at my soul.
Shaking, trembling,
no way out,
no reason for my angst.
Yet I can't find a way,
to ease my troubled soul.
Fighting through seems so hard,
yet what can I do?
I breathe in yet as I try,
I'm gasping for my breath.
The fear only increases
within each new pant.
How to ease my troubled
psyche,
how to calm my soul.
Little did I know,
that this was just the start.

I am a Woman

I am a woman,
A feminist too.
Men think I'm nothing,
A nuisance that gets in the way.
We love, we give,
Others so much,
More than we give to ourselves.
A shoulder to cry on,
Needs we have are ignored.
I am a woman,
And beautiful too.
Maybe you've seen me before.
Putting my heart on the line,
Reaching for all that I can.
Often I flounder,
Understanding I crave.
Driven to succeed.
I am a woman,
And powerful too.
Mistake me for no one else.
Serve no one, but yourself.
Take what is yours,
Reach for the stars,
Own who you are.
Never surrender,
Good enough and more.

I forgot to tell you...

I forgot to tell you I loved you,
that fateful night on the phone.
That one brief call,
that I didn't know,
would be the last we spoke.

I forgot to tell you,
how much you meant to me.
The years we spent,
the fun we had,
can never be exchanged.

I forgot to tell you,
how grateful that I am,
for all the times you bailed me out,
but mostly for the
love you always showed.

I forgot to tell you,
a million other things.
Time goes by,
and as it does,
the list increases by day.

I wish I remembered to tell you,
all the little things,
that in my heart
I feel for you,
words cannot define.

So, I will start to tell you,
in my heart
and in my dreams,
the words
I left unsaid.

So, from here on out,
each night as I lay,
in my bed.
I will say those three words
that haunt me to this day.

I Told You I Would Find You.

You came into my life
most unexpectedly.
And slowly took my heart.
Your quiet ways,
your thoughtful eyes,
showed more than
words can say.
Inch by inch,
and brick by brick,
a friendship we had built.
Based on love of written word
you became my one.
A kindred spirit,
I had never known,
or even thought possible.
Your humor and intelligence,
you had me at hello.
Yet darkness reigned,
inside of you,
and you never let on.
The closer we got, the less I saw
what I should have seen.
I saw what I wanted to
and what you
needed to project.

Never wanting to really see
the demons you hid from me.
We never knew,
what could have been.
For no matter what,
we knew deep down,
some walls were there to stay.
Then that fateful day arrived,
I told you I was going away.
Not for long, not forever,
these words you never heard.
I told you I would find you,
I told you to find me.
You smiled and said you would;
and again I didn't see.
I never saw the demons winning
even on that final day.
When you couldn't
write those final words to me.
I had hope that I
would find the love
I had always sought.
I was blind,
I denied to see beyond
your spoken words.
What you must have felt,
when you decided to leave,
I will never really know.
I'm sorry that I didn't find

a way to tell you to hang on.
The day I heard, I didn't think
anything could hurt so much.
The dagger of your leaving me
still pierces at my soul.
My kindred spirit, my other half,
how could you leave me?
I told you I would find you,
why could you not believe?
Every day, I think of you,
with sadness in my heart.
Blowing kisses to the sky,
or railing at you still.
My friend, my love, my confidante,
you never liked to see me cry.
If only you knew how many tears
I shed for you today.
I'll never forget who you are,
or what you mean to me.
Be at peace, my dear
dear friend,
I'll find you again
one day.

Naive

I am young,
some say naïve.
Because I see the best.
I see the world, I feel the pain.
I hear the children cry.
I've been hurt,
I've been content,
I'm not so naïve.
All of my life,
I have strived for peace.
But it is not good enough.
I still see tears,
no, I am not naïve.
I use hope,
to get through pain,
my dreams are filled
with warmth.
Don't call me naïve,
call me a dreamer
of what this world can be.

Not all who wander are lost

I once was lost,
but now I'm found,
lyrics of a song.
But what does
"lost" really mean,
and can one
really be "found".
A wanderer's soul,
a gypsy heart,
lies inside of me.
The urge to be
free as leaves
falling from a tree.
Being lost doesn't
always mean,
directions never found.
But loss of dreams
or loss of hope,
can lead to hate and doubt.
So, when you hear
me say the words
I'm lost,
I can't find my way.
Perhaps they mean
something more,
than the surface words
they seem to be.

Faraway Land

My soul, so tortured,
by demons inside,
telling me I'm no good.
A lifetime of fighting,
of trying to live,
beyond what
this fear allows.
Always dreaming,
always afraid,
to make all these
dreams alive.
That even when,
a wish comes true,
I am only able to sigh.
I woke up today,
another year older,
in a faraway land.
It wasn't a dream,
not any longer,
today I made it a truth.
I stare at the mountains
of this magical place,
and finally, I feel alive.
the demons are there,
buried inside,

today I won't let them free.
I'll continue to fight them day by day.
But at this moment,
with tears in my eyes,
my soul can finally be free.

www.ingramcontent.com/pod-product-compliance
Lightning Source LLC
Chambersburg PA
CBHW051748130826
49812CB00033B/1053
9789357440400